T0379248

SCIENTIFIC AMERICAN | EDUCATIONAL PUBLISHING

SCIENTIFIC AMERICAN INVESTIGATES EARTH SCIENCE
HOW PRECIOUS METALS FORM

BY MEGAN QUICK

Published in 2026 by The Rosen Publishing Group
in association with Scientific American Educational Publishing
2544 Clinton Street, Buffalo NY 14224

Copyright © 2026 Rosen Publishing Group

Cataloging-in-Publication Data

Names: Quick, Megan.
Title: How precious metals form / Megan Quick.
Description: Buffalo, New York : Scientific American Educational Publishing, an imprint of Rosen Publishing, 2026. | Series: Scientific American investigates Earth's resources | Includes glossary and index.
Identifiers: ISBN 9781725352797 (pbk.) | ISBN 9781725352803 (library bound) | ISBN 9781725352810 (ebook)
Subjects: LCSH: Precious metals–Juvenile literature. | Mines and mineral resources–Juvenile literature.
Classification: LCC TS729.Q53 2026 | DDC 622'.342–dc23

Designer: Michael Flynn
Editor: Megan Quick

Portions of this work were originally authored by Julia McDonnell and published as *How Precious Metals Form*. All new material in this edition is authored by Megan Quick.

Photo credits: Cover, p. 1 RHJPhtotos/Shutterstock.com, p. 5 (coins) Aleksey Mnogosmyslov/Shutterstock.com; p. 5 (gold medal) fifg/Shutterstock.com; p. 7 White Space Illustrations/Shutterstock.com; p. 8 Bjoern Wylezich/Shutterstock.com; p. 9 Widy Amelia Putri/Shutterstock.com; p. 11 Gemstones By Boat/Shutterstock.com; p. 13 courtesy of NASA; p. 15 (solar system) Siberian Art/Shutterstock.com; p. 15 (Saturn) 24K-Production/Shutterstock.com; p. 17 Kateryna Kon/Shutterstock.com; p. 19 Jason Edward Dudley/Alamy Stock Photo; p. 20 Nanang Sugi /Shutterstock.com; p. 21 David Hayes/Alamy Stock Photo; p. 23 Inc/Shutterstock.com; p. 25 Alexey_Rezvykh/Shutterstock.com; p. 27 Ravital/Shutterstock.com; p. 29 Cloudy Design/Shutterstock.com.

Some of the images in this book illustrate individuals who are models. The depictions do not imply actual situations or events.

All rights reserved. No part of this book may be reproduced in any form without permission in writing from the publisher, except by a reviewer.

Printed in the United States of America

CPSIA compliance information: Batch #CSSA26. For Further Information contact Rosen Publishing at 1-800-237-9932.

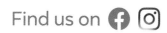

CONTENTS

EARTH'S SPECIAL METALS 4

THE SCIENCE OF METAL. 6

A RARE FIND 10

THE SOLAR SYSTEM IS BORN 12

BURIED TREASURES 16

DISCOVERING DEPOSITS 18

ALL ABOUT ORE 20

DIGGING AND DRILLING 22

SEPARATING AND REFINING 24

JEWELRY, MONEY, AND MEDICINE. 26

PRESERVING PRECIOUS METALS 28

GLOSSARY 30

FOR MORE INFORMATION 31

INDEX 32

Words in the glossary appear in **bold** type the first time they are used in the text.

EARTH'S SPECIAL METALS

If a runner finishes first in a race, they might win a gold medal. If you do well on a school paper, you might get a gold star. Why is gold so special? Gold is rare, valuable, and shiny! These are some of the qualities of precious metals.

Gold is not the only precious metal. Others include silver, platinum, and palladium. Like most metals, precious metals are hard, conduct electricity, and are found in Earth's crust. But each one has other traits that set it apart. Precious metals are not simply shiny objects. They have a broad range of uses including art, **technology**, and medicine.

FUN FACT

THE OLYMPIC GOLD MEDAL IS NOT PURE GOLD! IT'S MAINLY MADE OF SILVER, WITH SOME GOLD ON THE OUTER LAYER. THE SILVER MEDAL IS ALMOST ALL SILVER.

Olympic gold metal

Gold is ideal for making jewelry and coins because it is soft and can be easily shaped and molded.

THE SCIENCE OF METAL

Metals are the most common type of chemical element. There are a total of 118 elements and more than 90 are considered metals. Like all matter, each metal is made up of tiny atoms. At the center of each atom is a nucleus made up of neutrons (particles with no charge) and protons (particles with a positive charge). Electrons (negatively charged particles) circle the nucleus. Each element has a different number of protons in the nucleus of its atoms.

Most metals have many "free" electrons, which move around easily. They help electricity move throughout metal. This is why metals are good conductors of electricity.

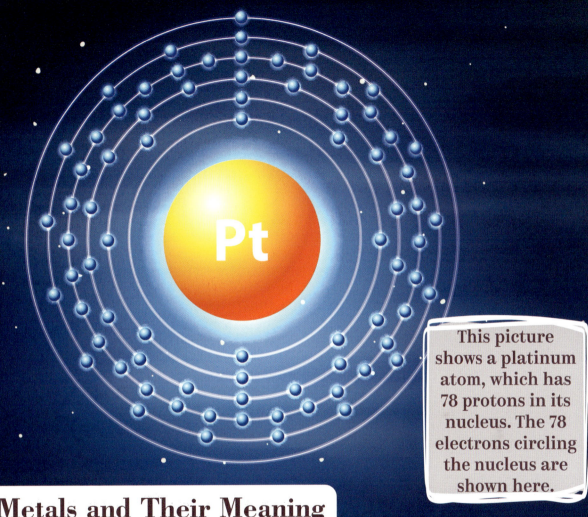

This picture shows a platinum atom, which has 78 protons in its nucleus. The 78 electrons circling the nucleus are shown here.

Metals and Their Meaning

The full list of precious metals includes gold, silver, platinum, ruthenium, osmium, rhodium, palladium, rhenium, and iridium. Some were named for their color, while other names come from how the metal was discovered. Ruthenium, for example, was discovered by a Russian scientist. The word "ruthenium" comes from the Latin word for Russia.

Another trait that gives precious metals their value is their stability. This means they don't react with chemicals easily, so they resist **oxidation** and don't **corrode**. Most are also ductile, meaning they can be stretched without breaking, and malleable, meaning they can be pressed and rolled into thin sheets. Precious metals usually have luster too. That means they reflect light, making them look shiny.

Precious metals are also transition metals, or metals whose atoms bond easily with those of other elements because of the arrangement of their electrons. Transition metals tend to be hard, strong, and have high melting and boiling points.

Periodic Table of Elements

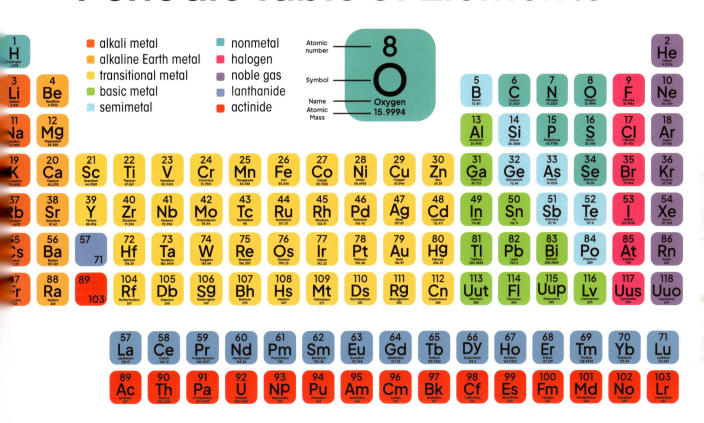

The periodic table, shown here, lists all of the elements. Notice the large group of transition metals (in yellow).

A RARE FIND

One reason for precious metal's value has nothing to do with science. When something is difficult to find, its value often increases. This is true of precious metals. Rhodium is the rarest of all precious metals. It's also the most valuable. At one point in 2023, it was worth $14,000 per ounce. At the same time, gold was $1,783 per ounce.

Metal's value can also decrease if it becomes more common. Years ago, aluminum was more precious than gold. Though plentiful in Earth's crust, it was costly to take from the ground. However, in 1886, new technology made aluminum mining easier. It became widely available, and aluminum's price dropped.

FUN FACT

GOLD IS RARE, BUT WELSH GOLD IS EVEN RARER! GOLD FROM TWO AREAS OF WALES IS THE SAME AS GOLD EVERYWHERE. BUT WELSH GOLD HAS ALMOST RUN OUT AND IS NO LONGER MINED, SO ITS VALUE HAS GREATLY INCREASED.

This bracelet is covered in a thin layer of rhodium. Jewelry is often coated with rhodium because it's shiny and protects jewelry from scratching.

THE SOLAR SYSTEM IS BORN

Precious metals are usually found in rocky areas below Earth's surface. How did they get there? Their formation probably began about 4.6 billion years ago. At that time, the solar system was just a cloud of dust and gases.

Something—perhaps a nearby exploding star—created waves, like ripples in a pond. The waves caused the cloud to collapse and form a spinning disk. As it spun, the matter within it became tightly packed together and finally became the sun. Following the sun's formation, bits of particles collected, bound by **gravity**. These particles were the beginning of the planets.

The sun formed from a collection of gas and dust.

The small particles came together to form larger and larger masses. Close to the sun, rocky and metallic dust collected to create the four planets that could withstand the nearby sun's heat: Mercury, Venus, Earth, and Mars. Farther from the sun, where solar winds and heat had less effect, gaseous and icy matter formed the planets we call gas giants: Jupiter, Saturn, Uranus, and Neptune. Moons, **asteroids**, and other space rocks formed as well.

All of the planets had grown out of the matter that had been floating about after the formation of the sun. Some of that matter would become precious metals.

FUN FACT

SCIENTISTS BELIEVE SATURN'S RINGS ARE LEFTOVER FROM WHEN SATURN FORMED. THEY MAY ALSO BE BITS OF MOONS, ASTEROIDS, AND OTHER SPACE OBJECTS THAT WERE RIPPED APART BY SATURN'S GRAVITY.

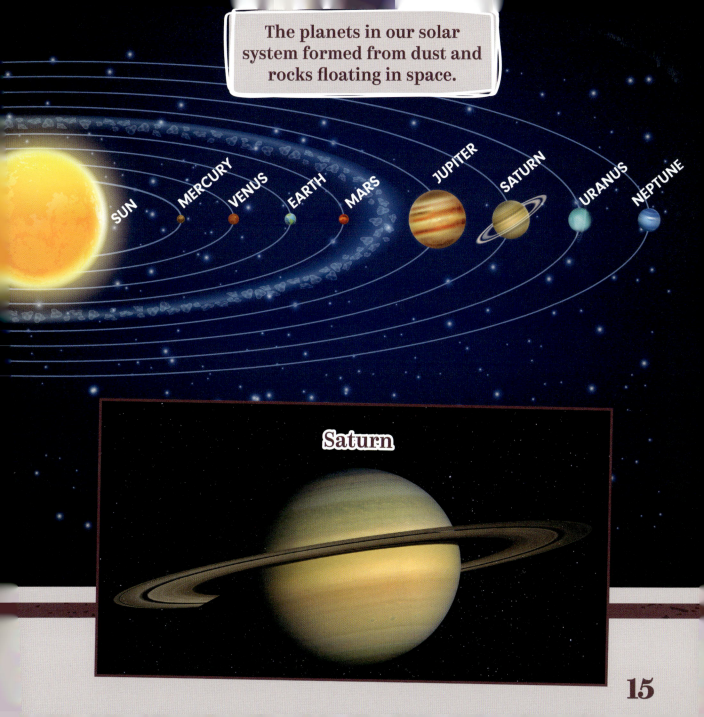

BURIED TREASURES

Earth's core formed first, with heavier matter—including metals—sinking to the center. Lighter matter rose to the surface, or crust. At first, Earth was so hot it was likely at least partly molten, or melted. When the planet cooled, precious metals were trapped in its inner layers. We currently don't have the technology to reach them.

We can reach precious metals in the crust, however. Scientists think that these metals probably reached Earth when asteroids crashed onto the surface. They believe that the metals landed in a molten sea, which trapped them and then became solid before the metals could sink to Earth's core.

Earth's Layers

CRUST

MANTLE

OUTER CORE

INNER CORE

Earth's core is made mostly of iron. Precious metals sank toward the core as the planet formed. There are more precious elements in the inner layers of Earth than in its crust.

DISCOVERING DEPOSITS

Earth's crust contains precious metals in their pure form as well as **alloys**. Some alloys occur in nature, while others are man-made.

Sometimes precious metals are found in lode **deposits**. These are veins or cracks within or between rocks filled with a metal. They're also discovered in placer deposits. These are pockets of metals that have been removed from another area by weathering and erosion. That means the bits are swept to a new location by the forces of water or wind. Placer deposits may be be found as nuggets or harder-to-spot flakes and grains. They are good sources of gold, platinum, and other metals and **gemstones**.

Tiny bits of gold, platinum, and sand, like these shown here, may be found in placer deposits.

Better Together

Alloys are a mix of two or more metals. By combining elements, alloys can create something even better! For example, silver easily tarnishes, or becomes dull or discolored. However, when copper is added to silver, it becomes sterling silver, which is used for medical tools and musical instruments that do not tarnish.

ALL ABOUT ORE

Ore is a combination of **minerals** found in Earth's crust. Ore can hold several different metals, which are a type of mineral. Silver is often discovered with lead and zinc, and gold can be found with copper and silver. Ore also contains rock. There may be a large amount of metal in ore, or a very tiny bit.

Ore contains enough metal to make it valuable for companies to collect it. Ore is a major source of precious metals, and mining companies depend on it. Once the ore has been removed from the crust, it's treated so the variety of minerals can be separated.

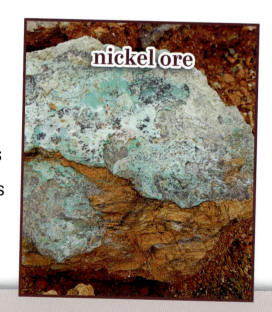
nickel ore

FUN FACT

PRECIOUS METALS ARE FOUND ALL OVER THE WORLD, INCLUDING ANTARCTICA. BUT THE METALS THERE WON'T BE COLLECTED ANYTIME SOON. IN 1988, THE ANTARCTIC TREATY PROTECTED THE CONTINENT'S ENVIRONMENT BY BANNING "ANY ACTIVITY RELATING TO MINERAL RESOURCES."

This piece of silver ore came from a mine in Arizona. It also contains the mineral quartz.

DIGGING AND DRILLING

Scientists test soil and rocks in an area to see if there are ore deposits. Once ore has been found, there are a few ways to reach it. In surface mining, rocks are drilled or blasted with explosives. The rocks are hauled away, and the metal is removed. Surface mining may also mean digging large pits and removing the ore inside.

When ore is deeper, companies use underground mining. They dig tunnels, sometimes over 1 mile (1.6 km) deep. Ore is cut, blasted, or drilled into pieces and carried to the mine's opening. Ore can also be found by sifting through sand and rock near rivers or beaches. This is called placer mining.

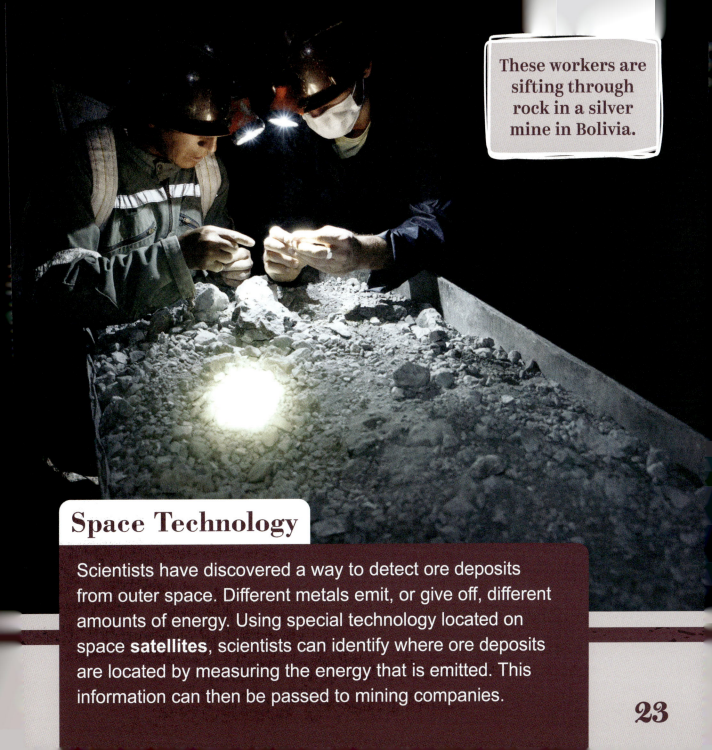

These workers are sifting through rock in a silver mine in Bolivia.

Space Technology

Scientists have discovered a way to detect ore deposits from outer space. Different metals emit, or give off, different amounts of energy. Using special technology located on space **satellites**, scientists can identify where ore deposits are located by measuring the energy that is emitted. This information can then be passed to mining companies.

SEPARATING AND REFINING

Ore deposits have been removed from the ground. Now what? Ore is usually crushed in order to expose the precious metals within it. Then the metal is separated from other matter, such as rock, minerals, and other metals. Next comes refining.

Refining removes **impurities** from metals. Depending on the type of metal, there are several ways to refine precious metal ore. During smelting, ore is heated until unwanted matter burns off or separates from metal. Chemical separation has to do with separating the metal by placing ore in a chemical solution. Another process uses special magnets to attract the metal and remove it from the rest of the ore.

Here, gold ore is being washed after being taken from the ground.

JEWELRY, MONEY, AND MEDICINE

Once precious metals have been refined, they are ready to be used. Precious metals have long been a sign of wealth and beauty. Jewelry, fashion, and art can all be created with various precious metals.

Precious metals have been used as money, too. They've been made into coins. They're also a way for countries to store wealth, usually in the form of gold or silver bars called bullion.

Precious metals are also used in medicines, dental fillings, cancer treatments, and medical tools. And in technology, they can be found in batteries, car parts, and all kinds of electronics.

FUN FACT

YOUR DOCTOR'S NEEDLES, BANDAGES, AND STETHOSCOPE, THE INSTRUMENT USED TO LISTEN TO YOUR HEARTBEAT, MAY BE LINED WITH SILVER! THIS PRECIOUS METAL CAN FIGHT OFF GERMS AND PREVENT SICKNESS.

The numbers on these bars of silver and gold bullion show that they are almost (99.9 percent) pure precious metal.

Saving the Planet

Some precious metals are good for the planet. When cars burn fuel, they emit gases such as carbon dioxide. These harmful gases play a major part in **climate change**. Today, most gasoline-powered cars have a part containing platinum, palladium, and rhodium. These metals cause a chemical reaction that reduces the amount of harmful gas sent into the atmosphere.

27

PRESERVING PRECIOUS METALS

While precious metals have many important uses, extraction methods can cause problems. Mining can upset the land, release chemicals into the ground and waterways, and harm wildlife. Sometimes conditions for mine workers are dangerous or unhealthy. But changes are being made to make mining safer for the **environment** as well as workers. Scientists are discovering new ways to create precious metals without mining.

Precious metals are rare, and the supply will not last forever. Yet we depend on them more and more for advances in science and medicine. We must take care of the supply we have in the earth and continue to develop technology for creating new precious metals.

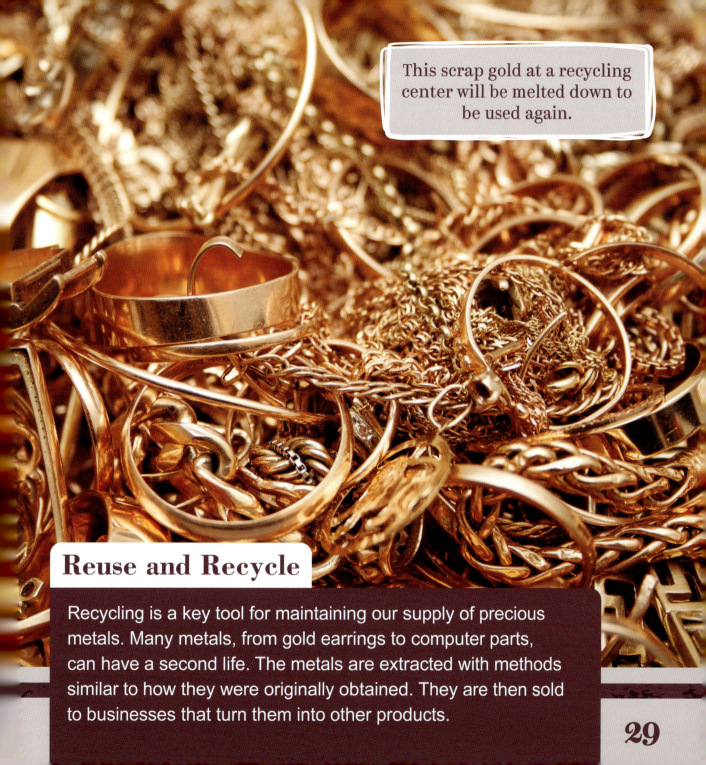

This scrap gold at a recycling center will be melted down to be used again.

Reuse and Recycle

Recycling is a key tool for maintaining our supply of precious metals. Many metals, from gold earrings to computer parts, can have a second life. The metals are extracted with methods similar to how they were originally obtained. They are then sold to businesses that turn them into other products.

GLOSSARY

alloy: Matter made of two or more metals, or a metal and a nonmetal, melted together.

asteroid: Any of the small rocky bodies in space found especially between the orbits of Mars and Jupiter.

climate change: Long-term change in Earth's climate, caused mainly by human activities such as burning oil and natural gas.

corrode: To slowly break apart and destroy a metal through a chemical process.

deposit: An amount of a mineral in the ground that built up over a period of time.

environment: The natural world in which a plant or animal lives.

gemstone: A mineral that when cut and polished can be used in jewelry.

gravity: The force that pulls objects toward the center of a planet or star.

impurity: Something unwanted that is mixed in with a substance.

mineral: Matter in the ground that forms rocks.

oxidation: The process of combining with oxygen.

satellite: An object that circles Earth in order to collect and send information or aid in communication.

technology: Using science, engineering, and other industries to invent useful tools or to solve problems. Also a machine, piece of equipment, or method created by technology.

FOR MORE INFORMATION

Books

Dingle, Adrian. *My Book of the Elements*. New York, NY: DK Publishing, 2024.

Dodd, Emily. *Geology*. New York, NY: Kingfisher, 2022.

Hinman, Bonnie. *Mining Techniques*. Minneapolis, MN: Abdo Publishing, 2024.

Websites

Britannica Kids: Metal
kids.britannica.com/kids/article/metal/390809
Read about the properties of metals, their history, and how they're extracted.

Ducksters: Gold
www.ducksters.com/science/chemistry/gold.php
Find out lots of fun facts about gold.

NASA Science Space Place: The Big Bang
spaceplace.nasa.gov/big-bang/en/
Discover more about the beginning of the universe.

Publisher's note to educators and parents: Our editors have carefully reviewed these websites to ensure that they are suitable for students. Many websites change frequently, however, and we cannot guarantee that a site's future contents will continue to meet our high standards of quality and educational value. Be advised that students should be closely supervised whenever they access the internet.

INDEX

alloys, 18, 19

bullion, 26, 27

copper, 19, 20

Earth's layers, 16, 17

electricity, 4, 6

elements, 6, 8, 9

formation of precious metals, 12, 14

gold, 4, 5, 7, 10, 18, 19, 20, 25, 26, 27, 29

jewelry, 5, 11, 26

lode deposits, 18

mining, 10, 20, 21, 22, 23, 28

ore, 20, 21, 22, 23, 24

palladium, 4, 7, 27

placer deposits, 18, 19

platinum, 4, 7, 18, 19, 27

refining, 24, 26

silver, 4, 5, 7, 19, 20, 21, 23, 26, 27

smelting, 24

recycling, 29

rhodium 7, 10, 11, 27

traits of precious metals, 8

transition metals, 8, 9

value, 10